D

The Untold and Untrue Story

LINUS KARP

With forewords by Zina Badran, Sam Carlyle, Deborah Frances-White, Elisabeth Ljunggren and Linda Paterson, and an afterword by Joseph Martin.

Reconnecting Rainbows Press

To team Pleasance,

We goofing love you

Ji Ke
xx

[signature]
xx

DIANA

Published in the UK by Reconnecting Rainbows Press

ISBN 978-1-915893-05-5

First edition, 2023

Reconnecting Rainbows Press CIC (14570208) is a community interest
company registered in the United Kingdom. All of our profits go back
into helping marginalised communities publish their works and tell their
stories.

www.reconnectingrainbows.co.uk

Linus Karp *(he/him)* is an actor, writer, theatre maker and full time princess. Originally from Sweden, he now resides in North London from where he runs Awkward Productions alongside his creative and life partner Joseph Martin. "Diana: The Untold and Untrue Story" is his second full length show, following "how to live a jellicle life: life lessons from the 2019 hit movie musical 'cats'". He is passionate about queer theatre, comedy and pizza.

CONTENTS

AN INTRODUCTION FROM LINUS KARP

Hello.

If you're reading this you've probably purchased my play script. Thank you. (If you've stolen it, then please hand it back and go directly to jail). Creating this show has been one of the great privileges of my life. I am thrilled that you are now able to consume my deeply stupid words.

As this is a story about the most iconic woman to ever live; I'd like the most iconic women from my own life provide to you with the introduction to the script. I give you Elisabeth, Linda, Sam, Zina and Deborah. My mother (responsible for introducing Diana adoration into my life), my mother-in-law (responsible for this story being created), two of my best friends (whose comedy, talent and creativity have helped make the show what it is) and my comedy hero. Such icons. Enjoy.

FOREWORD BY LINDA PATERSON

My Path to International Theatre Stardom or How to Turn Two Dodgy Books, a Watch, a Plaster Bust and a Teaspoon into a Hit Play.

Mysterious packages had been arriving for me over several months with no word of explanation. They had one thing in common. They all featured my late contemporary - Diana, Princess of Wales.

After much head-scratching and bemusement it transpired that they had all, of course, come from Joe and Linus, our delightfully mischievous and completely crackers son and son-in-law-to-be (can you get a move on with that wedding please?). Fast forward to 2021 when Diana and I should both have reached our 60th birthday, mine being three months before hers. Sadly that milestone was not to be for her but, had she reached it, I can't imagine that she'd have had a better gift from anyone than my gift from Linus.

On April 14th the whole family - Martin, Ruby, Bryn, Jay, Joe, Linus and I - sat in the garden and performed what has turned into the glorious piece of mayhem you now hold in your hand. Fast forward once more to November 12th 2022 when I found myself onstage at The Pleasance Theatre in London, watching Linus crawl out from between my knees to begin one of the very first performances.

I had become mother to Diana. The circle was complete. It only remains for me to become mother-in-law to Linus. Please buy this script and get me one step closer. Joe and Linus, thank you. I couldn't love you more or be more proud of you. Always stay exactly who you are. But married.

Mum x

FOREWORD BY SAM CARLYLE

I lived with Linus and Joseph for a year. The day after we moved in, we went for a lovely afternoon walk. On this walk, they both encouraged me to climb a rather large tree and also eventually helped me down when I got stuck; after taking some photos of course. That's the kind of people they are; encourage you to take big risks and support you if things go wrong. They very quickly became two of the most important people in my life.

As individuals, they are both kind and generous kick-ass creatives. Together, they are a tour de force. 'Diana' is proof.

Linus is an exceptionally talented storyteller. He has a keen eye for detail and a real gift for comedy; he never misses a beat. Linus's level of passion for creating silly and infectious theatre is only matched by Joseph's unwavering support. Joseph's ability to learn a new skill or talent to a professional standard is enviable. They are multi-talented and execute each of these roles with such flair, it elevates the entire product (I mean, Camilla never looked so good).

'Diana' is just over an hour of unbridled joy. The fun the two of them have created is infectious. My mouth ached from laughing, even watching it for the fifth time. It is camp and queer and makes really important statements, before diving back into the ridiculousness of this untold and untrue story.

Oh, and music and choreography is sensational.

I think Diana herself would've been thrilled with this outrageous telling of her story. I can only hope that one day Linus and Joseph turn their hands and brains to tell my story in a way only they can. What a privilege that would be. Maybe just a couple more costume changes though...

FOREWORD BY ELISABETH LJUNGGREN

Since my teenage years I have been fascinated by Lady Di, her irresistible charm and personality. The tragic life that created one of the greatest icons of our time. Her eyes, hair, smile and style will never fail to move us. The star who, far too young, ended up in an unhappy marriage that shaped her life. How we'd love to make right her story and give her a happy ending.

The beautiful and brave Diana who, despite coming from an upper-class background, was not ready for the stiff life that awaited with the Windsors. She wholeheartedly engaged in issues affecting the weaker in society and had a unique ability to connect with others. The People's Princess. Supporting AIDS patients and contributing in the fight against landmines. After her divorce she became prey for the tabloid press.

Diana's main task had been to provide heirs, now she moved on to be a voice for those excluded by society. Beloved Diana, you are immortal. That fatal day in August '97 changed the world. The Brits mourned deeply and £27 million worth of flowers were placed at the royal palaces. "Goodbye England's Rose", Elton John sang at the funeral. I still can't hear the song without shedding tears. "Your candle burned out long before your legend ever will".

Thank you, Linus, for redressing the events in Diana's life through this extraordinary show. You're letting her tell her story and live her life fully in all colours of the rainbow. I think we can all imagine Diana's smile at the less than flattering portrayals of Charles and Camilla. Her untold stories, and the untrue ones too. Who would she have been today? Full of life, beautiful and brave. A voice for equality and fairness. An advocate for queer rights and unconditional love. Linus, thank you for a remarkable story. Diana, you are forever in our hearts.

Elisabeth Ljunggren, proud mother and Diana fan.

FOREWORD BY ZINA BADRAN

Not gonna lie. I Googled 'foreword'. I mean. Of course, I knew what it was. But not quite. Something I always flitted past and never read. It's written by someone other than the author that tells readers why they should read the book. Ok. This, I can do! As I'm not only an expert in the misuse of punctuation and grammar but also in all things Linus.

Who *is* this tall, awkward being that I saw for the very first time in our very first improv class? Could I have imagined that this person would be *such* fabulousness? The transition from polite, normal conversation to conversation that would get us both cancelled in the blink of an eye should anyone ever eavesdrop on us or our WhatsApp's get hacked; was so seamless, that we simply looked at each other one day and thought, WTAF. How *did* this happen?! Well. It did. And what a joy. I'm not sure this has anything to do with why you should read the play but I have five hundred words to fill (minimum).

And so, I discovered the weird and wonderful brain of Linus Karp. The brain that liked the 2019 film Cats. Sorry, not liked, *LOVED*. Like, he actually really loves it. Only *this* brain would get the inspiration to write a play from a 2.8 on IMDB film. Only *this* brain could create something positive from one of the most traumatic experiences of my life. I have only just forgiven him for taking me to the cinema to watch it. Only *this* brain could create a *Jellicle Name Generator* consisting of *Spunky Tugger the Chest Infection Cat* and make it go viral.

And so, before we get to the role of a lifetime for any actor, that I had the honour of being offered in *Diana the Untold and Untrue Story;* let's hear it for the play *Priti Patel Destroyed Our (gay) Wedding.* A moment's silence for that which never saw the light of day. Guess who would be playing Priti... Yes, me. The brown friend. Fortunately, I did not have to mourn the loss of this role for too long; that I would have gone totally method for by the way, I looked her up on You Tube and everything. Because with one hand Linus may have tooketh away... but with the other... he gave... GOD. God!!

I said I was happy to grow out my beard but was told it was a sassy female God. Oh! Fun! And we'll (shout out to Joseph Martin in 'we') get you a cute outfit too. Woo! It was gorgeous. Can I keep it?! No. Linus wants to wear it in his free time. Oh. Fair play. Can I borrow it every now and then? Of course! Splendid! Smiles all round. When it came to filming the role, I had an injured knee and hobbled all the way to north London in my car. No way was I going to miss out on putting God on Spotlight.

And so, as I excitedly exceed my five hundred words; haven't written this much since uni, I say to you... YOU SHOULD READ THIS BOOK SLASH PLAY. Why?... Because... it comes from the same brain I mentioned earlier. The playwright realised he looked like Diana and then wrote a play about it. It may have been slightly more complicated than that. But Mr. Karp had some extraordinary ideas about a most beloved and extraordinary woman; and wrote and performed an extraordinary play that I'm certain is making her chuckle up there every time it's performed. And if you're easily offended, don't watch Cats xx

FOREWORD BY DEBORAH FRANCES-WHITE

When I was asked to write a foreword to a story both untold and untrue, I felt very honoured to be accepting this most unusual of rabbits down the most alluring of holes. This play, like the Linus who wrote it, doth make Alices of us all. The Looking Glass we enter together as we assemble as an audience or open the first page of the text is both queer in that it is curiouser and curiouser and queer in that it allows us to rest our dullest assumptions and obligations for an hour.

What a relief to put down the luggage that is the heavy, ordinary norms and arbitrary, drab expectations of the every day and spend time in this tipsy-turvy, Karpian world of farcical frocks and titillating tragedy. Audience members step into the dream and take roles in this parallel cartooniverse, playing mothers and lovers and archbishops, oh my!

You, dear reader, will greedily take all the parts for yourself or perhaps dish them out at your next dinner party to your luckiest guests. In doing so, you become the teller of this untold story and find the truth in this untrue tale. There is an old Jewish proverb - there's nothing truer than truth but story. That's why we love it and thirst to live it. There is fact in fiction and veracity in whimsy.

This text blurs the shady edges of a story we know and many of us lived through. Within it you will hear a beating heart that pounds with a rhythm asking why Diana the Princess of Wales and the queer community seem so magnetically drawn to each other. Her compassion and insistent connection are alive here on the page in dangerous humour and surprising poignancy.

If Diana is Queen of Hearts, the recklessly talented Linus Karp is her representative on earth keeping us all feeling loved up, defiant and gay in our revenge dresses.

Page One - you're a princess. Permission to proceed.

For Linda, your birthday present now has a life of its own!

For Joseph, the love of my life without whom none of this would be possible.

And, of course, for Diana.

| 1 |

Credits

This show opened at The Pleasance Theatre (Downstairs) in London on 8th November 2022. The cast and creative team were as follows:

DIANA

Linus Karp (he/him)

CHARLES/CAMILLA/CAPTAIN SIR TOM MOORE/PADDY/PRE-SHOW ANNOUNCEMENT/OSCARS PRESENTER/KING OF NORWAY

Joseph Martin (he/they)

THE QUEEN

Geri Allen (she/her)

GOD

Zina Badran (she/her)

Writer, Co-Director, Producer

Linus Karp (he/him)

Co-Director, Producer, Additional Material, Stage Manager

Joseph Martin (he/they)

Designer

Amy Pitt (she/her)

Choreographer

Sam Carlyle (she/her)

Composer, Graphic Designer

Wez Maddocks (he/him)

LX Designer

Ebbe Rodtborg (he/him)

Photography, Videography

Dave Bird (he/him)

Video Editor

Daniel Boylett (he/him)

Drag and Makeup Artist

Carrot (they/them)

Puppetry Artist

Tara Boland (she/her)

BSL Interpreter

Nicola Williams (she/her)

PR

Franky Lynne (she/her) and Hannah McEwen (she/her)

from Chloé Nelkin Consulting

| 2 |

Cast & Audience

CHARACTERS

These are the primary roles in the show, played by two or more live actors and puppeteers or pre-recorded videos.

DIANA – to be played by live actor on stage

CHARLES – a cardboard cut-out and pre-recorded voiceover

CAMILLA – a human sized rag doll (controlled by a live puppeteer) and a pre-recorded voiceover

QUEEN – actor in pre-recorded videos

GOD - actor in pre-recorded videos

CAPTAIN SIR TOM MOORE – a 2D picture on screen and pre-recorded voiceover

PADDY – controlled and voiced by a live puppeteer

PRE-SHOW ANNOUNCEMENT - live voiceover provided by the Stage Manager

OSCARS PRESENTER – live voiceover provided by an actor

KING OF NORWAY - live voiceover provided by an actor

4

AUDIENCE ROLES

Before the show starts audience members are given role cards to play the following parts in the show. They are not given any lines in advance.

DIANA'S MUM
DIANA'S DAD
DIANA'S NANNY
DIANA'S PRIMARY SCHOOL TEACHER
DIANA'S DRAMA TEACHER
POOR SERVANT
ARCHBISHOP
GAY FAN 2
LANDMINE
CORGI
GAY SCIENTIST

The following audience roles Diana will select audience members for during the performance.

WILLIAM'S NANNY
HARRY'S NANNY
GAY FAN
MYSTERY MAN

| 3 |

Playscript

Diana: The Untold and Untrue Story

BY LINUS KARP

1

The stage is empty. The lights dim but stay on.

PRE-SHOW ANNOUNCEMENT: Good evening and welcome to [*insert name of venue*]. This is an update on tonight's performance. Due to the indisposition of Kristen Stewart, Emma Corrin and Elizabeth Debicki, the role of Diana will be played by Linus Karp. Some other roles will also be played by you, yes you, the audience. Your lines will appear on the screen, like this.

> *Timed with the line the following text appears on screen: "Your lines will appear on the screen, like this."*

PRE-SHOW ANNOUNCEMENT: These roles are uncontracted, unpaid and obligatory. They are to be played with aplomb, confidence and, above all, fun. To signal your agreement please whoop and cheer now.

> *Audience whoops and cheers.*

PRE-SHOW ANNOUNCEMENT: A bit louder.

> *Audience whoops and cheers louder.*

PRE-SHOW ANNOUNCEMENT: Thank you, and enjoy the show.

Blackout. Projection shows us moving through the clouds. An angelic sound is heard as the image changes to pink, divine clouds that circle around. A voice is heard.

DIANA: *(offstage until stated)* Hello. It is I. Lady Di. Calling from heaven. Do you know my true story, people of [*name of venue*]? Well, yes you probably do. I know how many me documentaries, films and musicals you've watched in the last year. But do you know the story that I'm going to share with you now? I very much doubt it. It's not the one told by the media, or the one in the history books, and it's definitely not… the truth. But it is my story. So. Let us start at the very beginning.

The screen shows the Big Bang taking place.

DIANA: Oh – not the very *very* beginning.

The video of the Big Bang rewinds quickly.

DIANA: But the important beginning. My beginning. In the kitchen of Diana's Mum and Diana's Dad in 1960.

2

A spotlight hits an X on stage. The screen reads "Diana's Mum and Diana's Dad get up on stage." The audience members playing Diana's Mum and Diana's Dad enter the stage and stand on the X. If required, the Stage Manager will prompt them. They read their lines as they appear on screen.

DIANA'S MUM: Good morning Diana's Dad.

DIANA'S DAD: Good morning Diana's Mum.

DIANA'S MUM: I think we should have another child.

DIANA'S DAD: Ok.

DIANA: Give it up for Diana's Mum and Diana's Dad!

The audience applaud as Diana's Mum and Diana's Dad get ready to retake their seats, when...

DIANA: But you're not finished quite yet...

3

Diana's Mum and Diana's Dad move back to the X. In front of the X lies a bed sheet. The screen reads: "Diana's Mum and Diana's Dad pick up the duvet cover and hold it as if they're in bed, but vertically." Once the 'actors' have followed the instruction the screen reads: "Yes, like that."

DIANA'S DAD: Oh yes.

DIANA'S MUM: Oh golly gosh!

DIANA'S DAD: Oh spiffing.

DIANA'S MUM: Oh yes this feels sooooooooooo…. good.

DIANA'S DAD: Let's have a child.

DIANA'S MUM: We already have two, lol.

DIANA'S DAD: Oops I forgot. Anyways I'm ejaculating now.

DIANA'S MUM: Good show.

DIANA: Give it up for Diana's Mum and Diana's Dad!

The audience applaud again as Diana's Mum and Diana's Dad get ready to sit back down, when…

4

DIANA: But don't sit back down yet. Because it is now... nine months later.

DIANA'S MUM: (*holding her pregnant belly*) OW! OUCH! OW! I'm in so much pain!

DIANA'S DAD: You can do it wifey! Push her out! Push her out like a candle in the wind.

DIANA'S MUM:
AOOOORRGGHGHHHHHOOOOWWWWWWWSSHHH-
HAAAAARRRGGHHHOOOOWWWWWWWW-
WOWOWOWOWOWOWOWOWOWAA*£$&£$FSH-
FGHGH$$£!!!!

> *A magical harp noise is heard. Diana has entered stage through the legs*
> *of her unsuspecting mother – thus being birthed.*

DIANA: Hello. It is I, Lady Di. I have been birthed.

DIANA'S MUM AND DAD: (*in unison*) Wow what a beautiful baby!

DIANA: I am baby. Thank you, mum and dad!

> *Diana's Mum and Diana's Dad sit back down in their seats.*

5

DIANA: Oh yes, those were the days, back in 1961 I was the most adorable baby. These days I spend my time in heaven, hanging out with my besties. Crocheting with Betty White. Watching "A Place In The Sun" with Captain Sir Tom Moore. Playing Uno with Vanessa Feltz. And I thoroughly enjoy it. But I am here with you today, good people of [*location*]. Let's go girls.

The instrumental intro of 'Man! I Feel Like A Woman' by Shania Twain plays for a couple of seconds.

DIANA: I'd just been birthed into this world – without even asking for it. And it wasn't always easy. I was one of four siblings and my beloved parents divorced when I was only 7. (*directed to Diana's Mum and Diana's Dad*) I'm sorry it didn't work out for you two. Despite the hardships I was still wildly privileged, beautiful and kind – let us hear some actual testimonials from my upbringing.

The screen reads: "Diana's Nanny stands up."

DIANA'S NANNY: Wow baby Diana is so good - she has already taught me how to avoid landmines on my way to work!

DIANA: You're welcome.

The screen reads: "Diana's Primary School Teacher stands up."

DIANA'S PRIMARY SCHOOL TEACHER: Wow child Diana is such a good girl – she's made everyone stop bullying the little gay boys. A true ally. We stan.

Diana gently hits her fist on her heart in solidarity. The screen reads: "Diana's Drama Teacher stands up."

DIANA'S DRAMA TEACHER: Wow student Diana is such a talented actor – she should definitely win an Oscar for playing Kristen Stewart in a biopic one day.

DIANA: The years passed and nothing very interesting happened. So all of a sudden I was, sort of, grown up. Then one day, a rather unexpected visitor came for tea.

Diana exits to cute fairy tale music.

Diana enters stage with a cardboard cutout – its back facing the audience. In time with music, she swings the cutout around and places it centre stage– it's revealed to be Prince Charles. He speaks through pre-recorded VO.

DIANA: Oh dear. hello there.

CHARLES: Hello, I'm Prince Charles, Prince of Wales.

DIANA: Jesus fucking Christ, I know who you are, you're very famous.

CHARLES: Haha, well, true that. Whatever being famous means.

DIANA: Well, me, a beautiful young lady Di, being here with you, a prince, in this stately home is a bit romantic – don't you think?

CHARLES: Ehm…well yes. Whatever stately home means.

DIANA: You're so awkward.

CHARLES: You have no idea.

Suddenly the lights go dark and red, and a loud monster growl is heard. Diana is horrified.

MONSTER VOICE: *(offstage)* Grrrooouugghh! CHARLESSSSS GGRRRaaahhhh.

CHARLES: Not now dear.

MONSTER VOICE: OKAYYY.

The lights go back to normal. A relieved but bemused Diana looks around, breathes and decides to go back to flirting.

DIANA: Anyway. I'm young, hot and single. Oh, I just dropped something on the floor.

Diana deliberately throws a polaroid picture on the floor.

CHARLES: I'll get it.

Diana stares at the cardboard Charles who doesn't move. Then she looks at the polaroid on the floor. Then back to the non-moving Charles.

Diana: Don't worry, I'll get it.

Diana bends down to pick up the picture in a way that ensures Charles gets a good view of her bum. She holds the picture up for Charles.

Charles: GASP! A bikini pic!

Diana slides the picture into cardboard Charles' cardboard breast pocket.

DIANA: Oops. Glad you like it, king.

CHARLES: Prince. Maybe we should date.

DIANA: Oh, how romantic. (*to audience, to show time passing*) We had quite a nice time together, the Prince and I.

Diana and Charles are laughing together.

CHARLES: Hahaha what a story Diana - you're so funny! I think you should write comedy shows!

DIANA: Oh... (*gives a knowing look at the audience*)

CHARLES: I've been thinking. You're still a teenager, I'm 30, and we've only just met. Therefore, it is time for us to take the next step.

DIANA: Oh gosh, omg. Do you mean what I think you mean?

CHARLES: I mean what I mean if that's what you mean. Whatever that means.

DIANA: I can't believe you mean it.

CHARLES: It's time you met my mother.

DIANA: Your mother?

CHARLES: My mother.

DIANA: Wow. Your mother. (*to audience*) Dear audience. His mother is not just any mother. She is the Queen.

Diana exits with Charles.

7

Queen music plays. The Queen appears on screen, against a backdrop of the interior of Buckingham Palace.

QUEEN: I am the Queen. I have been the Queen for a very long time, and I shall continue to be the Queen for (*checks watch*) 41 more years!

Screen calls for Poor Servant to enter stage. Audience member playing Poor Servant stands on the X.

QUEEN: You have made your last mistake here, peasant!

POOR SERVANT: B-but your majesty, I'm so sorry, I shall do better in the future, I promise.

QUEEN: Quiet! I've had enough of your lame excuses! Off with their head!

The Poor Servant screams as they're dragged away.

QUEEN: Who's next then, lads?

Diana and Charles enter.

CHARLES: Oh, hi your majesty mama.

QUEEN: Good day your royal highness son. Hmmm. Who's this lady?

DIANA: Oh, your majesty, I'm just me, Lady Diana Spencer, Queen of Hearts and the People's Princess.

QUEEN: Diana eh… What are we going to do with you…

CHARLES: You see, Diana and I have spent some time together mama.

DIANA: That is the sweetest thing you've ever said, Charles.

QUEEN: I see. One was rather worried that you'd want to marry that dreadful ghoul for a while.

CHARLES: She has a name! Camilla is not a ghoul… She's a beautiful woman.

DIANA: What?!

QUEEN: What?!

CHARLES: Uh, what I meant to say is… ehm..

DIANA: …yes?

QUEEN: …yes?

CHARLES: …ehm… I like… Diana and…

DIANA: …oh?

QUEEN: …oh?

CHARLES: ...ehm... I think that maybe she could make me quite happy and...

DIANA: ...what?

QUEEN: ...what?

CHARLES: ...ehm... maybe we should get married!

DIANA: Oh golly! Married!

QUEEN: Married!?!

DIANA: Oh gosh – this is the happiest moment of my life! You're the prince and I'm just a little lady who works in a nursery. (*to audience*) I know we haven't covered that so far in the story, but I am.

QUEEN: So you two are in love then?

DIANA: Well, yes. I am in love, very much so.

CHARLES: Yes. Whatever in love means.

Diana fades away from stage as Charles' final line echoes.

8

St Paul's Cathedral. Millions of people are gathered, dressed for a party, and not just any party. Paparazzi everywhere, flashes go off. Love is in the air – it's the wedding day! Trumpets play as the screen calls for the audience member playing the Archbishop to enter stage. The Stage Manager hands over a big Archbishop hat for the Archbishop to wear.

ARCHBISHOP: *(slowly and grandly)* We are gathered here today to marry Prince Charles Philip Arthur George Windsor, and England's Rose, Lady Diana.

QUEEN: *(offstage)* Wait just a minute!

The lights snap dim as the Queen music plays. The Queen appears on the screen.

QUEEN: I am the Queen. Do you not realise that as the Queen, which I am, the Queen, I am also the Head of the Church of England? I outrank you Mr. Archbishop! I shall lead this service!

ARCHBISHOP: Oh, your majesty, if that's what you wish then of course we will-

QUEEN: Off with his head!

The Archbishop is dragged off, kicking and screaming. The Stage Manager takes the hat back. The Queen puts it on instead.

QUEEN: Yes hello, it is me, the Queen. We are gathered here today to marry my little boy Prince Charles to Lady Diana. *gasp* Wow, look at Diana in that dress!

Diana enters wearing a stunning wedding dress.

DIANA: Oh, this little thing?

Screen calls for the crowd to applaud and swoon. Diana walks across the stage, waving at the crowd. The train to her dress keeps on coming – it's 10m long.

QUEEN: Now walk her down the aisle Diana's dad.

Diana's Dad gets up and starts walking Diana down the aisle.

DIANA'S DAD: I'm so happy I get to walk you down the aisle, despite your mother leaving me.

The screen calls for Diana's Mum to wave at them – and then for her to lean over and kiss her new husband.

DIANA'S DAD: I can't believe she's moved on already...

DIANA: Shut up and walk me down the aisle dad, today's not about you.

DIANA'S DAD: Sorry...

They reach the front where Prince Charles stands waiting.

DIANA: *(to her dad)* That's enough of you now.

Diana's Dad sits back down.

QUEEN: Good day to you all. I am the Queen. You're all gathered here today, Lords, Ladies, all the beautiful proper people, the riff raff at the back, and everyone at home – to witness two young people get happily married ever after, or until Camilla or a car crash do they part. Now little Charlie boy, repeat after me. I, Prince Charles:

CHARLES: I, Prince Charles.

QUEEN: Hereby promise to take you Lady Di for better or for worse, be by your side and to use my royal sceptre to provide an heir to the throne.

CHARLES: *(Chuckles awkwardly)* Yes to all of the above ma. Whatever sceptre means.

QUEEN: It means your penis Charles. Now your turn. I, Lady Di:

DIANA: I, Lady Di-

QUEEN: Promise to be a perfect wife and provide the Queen, that is me, I am the Queen, with grandsons.

DIANA: Yes to that and also to be a fashion icon and to hold hands with gay men with AIDS – no one has really done that before, there's still such a stigma around both AIDS and homosexuality, and any other form of queerness for that matter and I really want to change that. I love queer people and I think it's important that we value and respect that community.

QUEEN: Whatever you say. Do you take each other?

DIANA: I do.

CHARLES: I do. Whatever I do means.

QUEEN: I now pronounce you Prince and Princess of Wales. You may kiss the bride.

Diana leans in for a kiss. Cardboard Charles doesn't move. Eventually Diana pulls him towards her and smooches.

QUEEN: May your days be blessed and may you, like me, live for 96 years. I am the Queen.

DIANA: I am so happy.

Happy, hopeful, playful fairytale music plays as Diana and Charles dance together. Diana throws herself at Charles who falls over. They laugh and spin round and round, until Charles throws up. Happy and in love, Diana embraces Charles.

9

Diana and Charles are together.

DIANA: Ah, married life. Oh Charles.

CHARLES: Oh Diana baby. This is nice. Talk dirty to me.

DIANA: Oh. Ehm… You're a parasite living on taxpayers' money.

CHARLES: Oh… Not like that.

A phone rings.

CHARLES: I'd better take this.

DIANA: No, just stay here with me.

The phone rings again.

CHARLES: But it could be important.

DIANA: What's more important than your wife Lady Diana Spencer, Princess of Wales? *(to audience)* that's me.

The phone keeps ringing. Diana sighs, walks off stage and returns with a litter picker holding a phone with a long phone cord coming off it. The cord extends into the wings of the stage.

CHARLES: Hello. Oh hiii there. Yeah. No, what really? Oh, how lovely.

In between each of Charles' lines loud growling noises can be heard through the phone.

DIANA: Who is it?

CHARLES: Oh, it's no-one…it's uhm the uhm the uhm the plumber.

DIANA: But why is the plumber calling the Prince of Wales? We have staff for that? And why do they have such a monster growl?

CHARLES: Ehhh…

The telephone growls even louder. Charles puts it back to his ear.

CHARLES: (*into the phone*) No sorry darling, I can't keep you waiting.

DIANA: Who are you calling darling?

CHARLES: Oh ehm… the plumber.

Excited growling on the phone.

DIANA: This is very sus.

The sus sound from Among Us plays.

10

Diana steps forward to address the audience.

DIANA: Things weren't as good as they should've been... Someone else had entered our relationship... who was this monster? I thought – maybe a child or two would save our marriage and get Charles back on track. So I got pregnant.

The 'Having a Baby' jingle plays: "Having a baby, having a baby. She is a lady, having a baby"

Diana holds her pregnant belly as she is pushing out a baby. She makes painful, giving birth noises.

CHARLES: Oh dear. Ehm. Oh. Push.

DIANA: I am pushing!

She pushes. Out comes a baby - Prince William.

CHARLES: Oh, he's bald.

DIANA: Oh – William – the heir. Aw, he's a right royal cutie.

Diana holds her newborn lovingly as she walks across the room looking at the audience. She stops in front of an audience member.

DIANA: You.

She hands the baby to the audience member.

DIANA: Raise him well.

Diana walks back centre stage and addresses the audience.

DIANA: Not long after we had our first son, Prince Charles and I, at least I think it was Prince Charles who was the father – had our second son.

11

The 'Having a Baby' jingle plays again: "Having a baby, having a baby. She is a lady, having a baby."

Diana is pushing out another baby. She makes more giving birth noises.

CHARLES: Oh dear. Ehm. Oh. Push.

DIANA: I am pushing!

She pushes. Out comes a baby with ginger hair - Prince Harry.

CHARLES: Oh, he's ginger.

DIANA: Oh Harry – the spare. Aw, he's a right royal cutie.

Diana holds her newborn lovingly as she walks across the room looking at the audience. She stares the audience down, judging the audience members with her eyes. She finally stops in front of one.

DIANA: You.

She hands the baby to the audience member.

DIANA: Raise him well.

Diana turns to the audience.

DIANA: We were a family. And we were happy.

12

The Screen reads: "The nannies come on stage. (If you are holding a baby you are a nanny.)" The audience members holding babies enter stage and stand next to Diana and Charles.

CHARLES: We are a family. And we are happy.

DIANA: So happy.

BABIES: (*voiced by nannies*) Gagagogo.

DIANA: Awww, they're so cute. My little nepo babies. We are a family.

CHARLES: Whatever family means.

Suddenly the lights go dark and red as thunder sounds and flashes cover the stage.

MONSTER VOICE: (*offstage*) GRROOOUGGHHH!!!

DIANA: what was that?

MONSTER VOICE: (*offstage*) GRROOOUUGHHH!!!!

DIANA: (*to audience*) Viewers, I must warn you. What you are about to see is horrifying, nightmare creating and vomit inducing. You'd do well to cover your ears, eyes, noses and souls. Or just leave the auditorium altogether. It is my extreme displeasure to introduce you to...

Camilla enters, she is a human sized puppet with long flinging limbs, buttons for eyes and an unsettling smile. She drags her body over the audience.

CAMILLA: GRAAOOAGHHHH!!! OH HELLO! (*She sits herself down onto a male audience member*) THIS SEAT TAKEN? MMMM YEAH! CAMCAM HORNY. MWAH.

DIANA: (*to audience*) This is the harbinger of doom and the mistress of chaos.

CAMILLA: (*runs over to another audience member*) OH A CHEEKY FITTY! (*She puts her head in the lap of the audience member and makes vulgar tongue noises*) GRRAAHH!

DIANA: (*to audience*) The nightmare of nightmares and the slag of death! This is... Camilla.

CAMILLA: GRAAAOOOAAAAAAAAAAAAAAAAAAHH!

Camilla spins and spins around and ends up centre stage.

DIANA: Oh gosh, Charles, why is it here?

CHARLES: Oh, hi Camilla! How are you?

CAMILLA: GRROOOUGGHHH!!! CAMCAM SEE BABIES!!!

DIANA: Charles, stop her, she can't see my babies! She'll eat them!

CHARLES: It's ok, she just wants to say hi, she's a very good friend you know.

DIANA: Friend!?

CAMILLA: GRROOUUGGGHHH!!! HELLO LITTLE BABIES BABYBEBEBEBEBE!! UUUHH! CAMCAM HUNGY!!!

DIANA: Oh dear. I don't think they like it. They're crying.

Diana gives the Nannies a knowing look to make them voice the babies crying.

CAMILLA: GRROOOUUUGGHHH!!! HUSH HUSH … SAY HI TO AUNTIE SLASH MISTRESS CAMCAM!! GRROOUUGHH!!

DIANA: Oh no, they're even hurting themselves, they're that upset.

Diana gives the Nannies a knowing look to make them imitate the babies hitting themselves.

DIANA: Oh no! Harry is so scared his todger's frozen! Nannies – take the babies out of here. Get them to safety.

The Nannies return to their seats.

13

DIANA: Oh no.

Diana dramatically throws herself on the floor.

DIANA: That wasn't good at all. There were three of us in this marriage, so it was a bit crowded. It was clear to me that Camilla wasn't going to go away. I had to make her see that Charles belonged to me. So I decided to do what all proper Brits do when needing to talk something through – I took her to the pub.

14

Diana steps forward and Camilla joins Diana's side.

DIANA: I'm at the pub, you can tell because I'm leaning on the bar and catching the barman's eye. *(to the OS barman)* Two G&Ts please... and what would you like Camilla?

CAMILLA: MOTOROIL!

DIANA: And a pint of motor oil please. *(pause)* Oh, I'll ask. Is Pepsi alright?

CAMILLA: BLEURGHARGHSCHGHG!

DIANA: Oh. A keg of Stella then.

Mimed drinks arrive. Diana sips her G&Ts, Camilla pours the keg over herself.

CAMILLA: WROUGHGRAGHRR!

DIANA: Oh Camilla you've made such a mess. Both here and in my marriage.

CAMILLA: BURRRRPPP.

DIANA: I was hoping we could talk about Charles. Woman to...ehm...woman..?

CAMILLA: YES! ME, WOMAN! GGRRRAAOOWWW.

DIANA: Ok. It's so... interesting to try and find out what the Prince sees in you.

CAMILLA: (*throws her legs open in the air*) GROOOOWWRR!

DIANA: Oh gosh.

CAMILLA: GRRAAUGHHHHUUURGHHHHHHSSHHHGGR-
RRUUUZZZZKKKHHHKKKTTT!!!!!

DIANA: I'm sorry, I didn't quite catch that?

CAMILLA: (*slower and clearer*) GRRAAUGHHHHUUURGHHH-
HHHSSHHHGGRRRUUUZZZZKKKHHHKKKTTT!!!!!

DIANA: What! You don't care if we're married, Charles is still yours? But you have your own husband Camilla – isn't that enough?

CAMILLA: GROOUUGHOUGHOU!!

DIANA: Now that I've given him an heir and a spare, he'll come right back to you!?

CAMILLA: GROOOUGHH! HEHEHEHEHEH!!

DIANA: (*firmly*) No!

CAMILLA: WUH?!?!

DIANA: I said no! Camcam bad! Camcam go back to her own husband. Camcam leave us alone!

CAMILLA: HAHAHAHA!! CAMCAM DOES AS CAMCAM WISHES!! WOOOAH! (*more human*) BY THE WAY, CAMCAM LEFT PURSE IN THE CAR.

DIANA: Alright, I suppose I'll pay.

CAMILLA: WUAH! CAMCAM WINS AGAIN. BLEEEAGGHHHGGHHHH!

> *Camilla flies off, leaving a despairing Diana behind.*

15

DIANA: Oh no.

Diana dramatically throws herself on the floor again.

DIANA: It really was a nightmare. Charles was inhumane. Camilla was inhuman. There were three of us in this solo show – so it was a bit crowded. I was so lonely and betrayed. Every time I wasn't in a room, this is what I believe happened in it.

16

Nightmare sequence. Diana watches in horror as Camilla enters stage and heads over to Charles.

CHARLES: Ahh, kiss me with your tongues.

CAMILLA: GRROOUGHMMMMMMMHHH! MAKE MONSTER LOVE TO ME CHARLES!

CHARLES: Ehm yes, oh yes I will, you're so not ladylike, unlike my wife, Lady Di.

CAMILLA: GRROOOGHH!! HAHA YES!

CHARLES: Mmmm. I just want to be reborn as a tampon inside of you.

CAMILLA: GROOUGH?! MATE! THAT'S A BIT VILE, EVEN FOR ME.

CHARLES: Oh... Sorry...

CAMILLA: JUST SHUT UP AND RAW ME!

Camilla and Charles have wild, disgusting monster sex.

DIANA: No!!

The sex nightmare stops.

17

DIANA: I just couldn't understand it. Imagine having this (*shows off her body*) and still not being faithful… And it wasn't just the infidelity that was terrible. Charles also couldn't cope with how popular I became. It was obvious that he was getting jealous all the time. Even when a sweet gay fan ran up to me in the street.

Diana walks over to an audience member and indicates that they are Gay Fan as their lines appear on the screen.

GAY FAN: Wow Diana we love you! You look so stylish and iconic!

DIANA: Oh thank you, that's very kind!

GAY FAN: Can I have a selfie?

DIANA: Of course you can.

Diana hands a disposable camera to Gay Fan and poses for a selfie with them.

GAY FAN: Woohoo! Love you Queen!

DIANA: Haha, I'm not queen… Yet.

CHARLES: (*from the background - boring, grumpy and awkward*) …hmpf… What about me…?

The screen calls for Gay Fan 2 to stand up.

GAY FAN 2: Omg, you're Diana! Can I have an autograph?

DIANA: Oh of course you can – I love the gays.

Diana takes out a signed photo, she kisses it and hands it over.

DIANA: Keep it.

GAY FAN 2: Slay Queen!

DIANA: Maybe I will...

CHARLES: (*from the background - boring, grumpy and awkward*) ...hmpf... What about me...?

LANDMINE: Hehehe, I'm a landmine and I'm going to blow up an innocent villager.

DIANA: No! You will do no such thing! I have already cleared you and all the other landmines away and made the world a much safer place.

LANDMINE: Oh darn. You truly are too good for this world.

DIANA: Yes I am.

CHARLES: (*from the background - boring, grumpy and awkward*) ...hmpf... What about me?!

LANDMINE: Who is that awkward dude?

CHARLES: No one cares for me!! Boohoo!!

DIANA: That's not true, I care for you very m-

CHARLES: I've had it, Diana. I'm going to go to the one who loves me – Camilla!!

Beat.

DIANA: Oh Charles don't go!

Diana reaches out towards cardboard Charles, who doesn't move.

DIANA: Stay here!

Cardboard Charles does not move.

DIANA: Don't storm off again!

Diana turns Charles around.

DIANA: Oh no. He's storming off again!

Diana walks cardboard Charles to the back of the stage.

18

DIANA: Oh no!

Diana throws herself on the floor yet again, more dramatically than ever. A single spotlight falls on her.

DIANA: I was so sad and lonely. And as if all that wasn't enough, wherever I turned there were paparazzi following me, all the time.

The screen reads: "The audience take out their phones and start photographing Diana. Flash is encouraged." Lights flash and we hear the sound of endless photos being taken. Diana runs across the stage, shields herself and tries to find somewhere away from the cameras.

DIANA: Oh no, even here in [*area or city of performance*]!! On the first row. On the back row. Show some respect! Even stage left. I can't go anywhere. Gosh! Just ghastly! Leave me alone!

The flashes stop.

DIANA: What to do? I had to speak to someone who might make Charles see sense again. Who could that be? Hmm… Maybe…

Diana exits.

19

The screen calls for Corgi to enter. The audience member playing the corgi enters, wearing a corgi mask. The Queen music plays – and the Queen appears on screen, knitting.

QUEEN: *(to the corgi)* Who's a good boy? Who's a good boy? Come to Mummy, come to Mummy who's a good boyyyy? *(she looks ahead and puts the knitting down)* I am the Queen. *(to the corgi)* Sit! *(she continues)* I have been the Queen for a very long time. *(to the corgi)* I said sit! *(continues)* and I shall continue to be the Queen for *(checks watch)* 30 years. *(to Corgi)* run along. Good boy.

The corgi goes back to their seat in the audience. Diana enters.

QUEEN: Oh hi Diana.

DIANA: Hi Mama.

Diana rushes up and hugs the Queen.

QUEEN: Oh dear. What did you call me?

DIANA: You said I could always call you Mama.

QUEEN: I never said such a thing. Grow up.

DIANA: Oh gosh.

QUEEN: So why are you here?

DIANA: I have some bad news. I'm afraid Charles is in his flop era. Things are really bad between us.

QUEEN: Is this your fault?

DIANA: I actually don't think us women should blame each other for the shortcomings of mediocre men.

QUEEN: (*pause*) This is your fault.

DIANA: No, but really –

QUEEN: The monarchy will never accept independent women speaking their minds. You are to blame.

DIANA: No, really you must listen to me, you old crone!

QUEEN: You are the reason the monarchy is in danger. Get out of my house! Or, I'll take your head off!

DIANA: Oh for fuck's sake!

QUEEN: Release the hounds!

> *The screen calls for the corgi to chase Diana around the stage. Diana runs round and round the stage, followed by the corgi.*

DIANA: Now he's chasing me on all fours!

> *The corgi gets down onto all fours.*

DIANA: And he's barking!

The corgi barks.

DIANA: *(stops running)* That's enough now. Good boy.

She pats the dog.

DIANA: Now roll over.

The corgi rolls over.

DIANA: Now run off.

The corgi returns to their seat.

DIANA: *(to audience)* That's when I realised – I could no longer surround myself with the royals. I needed to be free. Free like a candle in the wind.

Diana exits.

20

Camilla enters to sexy 90's RnB music. She "flirts" with audience members as she passes them. She brings Charles onto the stage.

CAMILLA: GRRGGHHH!! MMM YEAAH! PUNISH ME KING!!

CHARLES: Ehm...oh... I'm not actually king yet I'm just-

CAMILLA: GGROOOUUUGHGHHH!!! SHOW ME PRINCE ALBERT!!!

CHARLES: Ehm...oh...no, I'm Prince Charles, you know that.

CAMILLA: GGRRROOOUUGHH!! PRINCE ALBERT MEANS YOU'VE DECORATED YOUR ROYAL – HUH – DIANA!?

Diana storms in, wearing an iconic post-Charles workout outfit – A Virgin Atlantic jumper, tight shorts and trainers.

DIANA: Well, hello there.

Camilla growls and starts levitating demonically.

DIANA: Oh no, Camilla, what are you doing!?

Camilla and Diana circle each other like boxers in a ring. Camilla attacks and they start fighting – an incredibly well choreographed fight. Cardboard Charles stands watching.

DIANA: Charles, do something!

Charles does nothing. Camilla and Diana fight even more – Camilla throws herself at Diana who's then had enough. She throws Camilla off, grabs her head and bashes it into the floor over and over..

DIANA: (*whilst bashing*) It didn't have to be this way, Camilla! We could've been friends!

HEAVENLY VOICE: (*offstage*) STOP!

The fighting stops.

CAMILLA: Hurgh!?

DIANA: What was that?

Angelic music plays as on the screen we see Captain Sir Tom Moore descend from heaven.

DIANA: Captain Sir Tom Moore!

CAPTAIN SIR TOM MOORE: Stop fighting. Get away from her.

DIANA: Oh Captain Sir Tom, you're so right! Violence is never the answer.

CAPTAIN SIR TOM MOORE: No, I just wanted you to move out of the way so that I could do this.

Sir Captain Tom Moore charges up and does a superpower move that sends Camilla flying across the stage.

CAPTAIN SIR TOM MOORE: Ha ha ha ha, game over.

DIANA: Well done Captain Sir Tom!

CHARLES: Oh… ehmm… uh… Diana listen, I…

DIANA: No, you listen. Keep your sausage fingers off of me. We're over. The day you become king will be a very sad day for this country. I can only hope I'm not around to see it. Dear Lord, what a sad little life, Charles. You ruined my life completely so you could have Camilla, and I hope you take some lessons in grace and decorum, because you have all the grace of a reversing dump truck without any tyres on. You're almost as pathetic as your nonce of a brother and I am no longer your wife – I am England's rose and you're about to learn that this rose… has thorns.

CHARLES: Oh… I…

DIANA: (*Turns to Camilla*) And as for you Camilla. I do pity you. Charles is terrible at making love.

CHARLES: Whatever making love means.

CAMILLA: GRROOOHHHH!! CAMCAM SAD!!

DIANA: I'm off. Bye bye.

CAPTAIN SIR TOM MOORE: I'll come with you Diana – you will never walk alone.

Triumphant music plays as Diana victoriously drags Charles and Camilla off stage.

21

Diana enters.

DIANA: I had unshackled myself from my marriage, and could finally talk about things that mattered – like GAY RIGHTS!

Cuts to the middle of Diana delivering a passionate speech.

DIANA: So, not only will I hold your hand, but I will hug you and tell you that you, as well as all queer people, deserve love, respect and happiness. We are tired of the Conservatives' lack of care for queer people, and as I'm talking to you today... *(beat)* from the late 80's... Surely this must be the end of people ever voting Tory. I dread to think what awful mess we'll be in 30 years from now otherwise. Queer issues and queer lives are important, and I will always champion them.

An 80's Gay anthem starts playing, Diana grabs a pride flag and starts dancing. On the screen we see a slide show of queer people expressing joy – a range of queer people and identities included.

LYRICS TO SONG PLAYING:
You're a friend of Di, you're a friend of Di
Whether gay, trans or bi
You're a friend of Di
You're a friend of Di, you're a friend of Di

Whether gay, trans or bi
You're a friend of Di

Defender of anyone who's queer
She's on our side, have no fear
She will hug you if you have AIDS
Love for us she has in spades

You're a friend of Di, you're a friend of Di
Whether gay, trans or bi
You're a friend of Di
You're a friend of Di, you're a friend of Di
Whether gay, trans or bi
You're a friend of Di

Defender of anyone who's queer
She's on our side, have no fear
She will hug you if you have AIDS
Love for us she has in spades

You're a friend of Di
You're a friend of Di
You're a friend of Di

The song ends with Diana posing powerfully.

DIANA: To get some time away from the royals and to focus on just being me, I travelled to (*in French*) Paris... That means Paris in French.

Diana exits.

22

The Queen music plays and the Queen appears on the screen, reading a newspaper.

QUEEN: *(reading aloud to herself)* Dear Miriam, my husband and I have been... *(calling over her shoulder)* Oh Philip, it is normal! *(spotting another story in the paper)* Hmmm... in Paris are you Diana...? Well, there's something you ought to know... No one puts the crown in a bad light or divorces out of my family. You will see...You will see...

23

French music starts playing. Diana enters in a sports car. She is wearing sunglasses and is smoking a cigarette – looking like a film star. She takes a blow of the cigarette and then throws it away over her shoulder. A badly drawn backdrop of Paris is seen on screen, the road constantly moving forward.

DIANA: Je ne regrette rien. Leaving Charles was the best thing I've ever done! Gosh I love driving in Paris. Look!

She zooms past the Eiffel Tower on the screen.

DIANA: The Eiffel Tower. Wow! The Arc de Triomphe.

She zooms past The Arc de Triomphe.

DIANA: Cool! Louvre.

She zooms past Louvre.

DIANA: Je t'aime. Baguette!

She zooms past a baguette.

DIANA: Yum!

24

The Queen in Buckingham Palace.

QUEEN: *(singing to the tune of Spiderman)*
Lady Di, Lady Di,
Does whatever a Lady Di does
Can she drive, through a tunnel,
No she can't, she will die.
Hahaaa!
Lady Di will die!

25

Diana driving in Paris. Diana takes a puff from a cigarette, then throws it away. An ominous looking tunnel appears on screen.

DIANA: What's that? A tunnel! I know, I'll drive into that tunnel!

26

The Queen in Buckingham Palace.

QUEEN: *(to camera)* Diana's going to drive IN to a tunnel... But she's not going to come out.

The Queen sips tea from a cup – the cup is Diana and Charles wedding memorabilia.

27

Diana driving in Paris. Diana takes a puff from a cigarette, then throws it away. She sticks her head out of the car window, hair blowing in the breeze.

DIANA: Oh I'm going to drive. Through the tunnel. Oui, oui, oui! (*to audience*) That means yes in French.

28

The Queen in Buckingham Palace.

QUEEN: I don't know if you've understood but I'm going to have Diana killed in the tunnel.

29

Diana driving in Paris. Diana takes a puff from yet another a cigarette, then throws it away.

DIANA: Just arriving at the tunnel! Hang on, I know who I haven't spoken to in a long time! My friends – the audience at [*name of venue*]. I'll call them on my new mobile phone; because they have become popular by now, so I have one.

Diana pulls out a 90's mobile phone with a long antenna. The screen instructs the audience to say:

AUDIENCE: Hello?

DIANA: Hello, it is I. Lady Di. Calling from Paris! How are you?

The screen calls for the audience to improvise a phone conversation. But before they have a chance to say too much Diana interrupts -

DIANA: Oh, I can't really hear you! I may be losing signal as I'm heading into a tunnel. Or do you think I should turn around?

The audience urges Diana to turn around. Adlib as necessary.

DIANA: Ok, I'll do as you say, I'll turn around. Nice speaking to you. Au Revoir! That means – oh they hung up.

Diana turns the car around and drives off. Extreme explosions can be seen in the tunnel.

30

The aftermath of the explosion. Diana enters stage. She takes off her sunglasses.

Silence.

DIANA: Phew. I had survived. And I didn't even know how lucky I was. But when I got back to my hotel room that evening – there was someone mysterious there, waiting for me.

During her speech Diana hands the sunglasses to a seemingly casually selected audience member.

DIANA: Gosh, it was so nice to catch up with the [*name of venue*] lot, I just wish they weren't such slags. GASP! A mystery man! Standing right there.

Diana points at the X on the stage and stares at the audience member she handed the glasses to until they stand on it. Lines for Mystery Man appear on screen.

MYSTERY MAN: Hello Diana.

DIANA: Who are you?

MYSTERY MAN: I am a mystery man working for MI5. I am not allowed to be here, but I need to tell you something. Even if that means breaking orders from my boss… the Queen.

DIANA: The Queen's your boss? Merde! (*to audience*) That means shit in French.

MYSTERY MAN: I must tell you something. Something shocking to YOU Diana, but not to YOU audience, because you already know it.

DIANA: (*to audience*) Have you been keeping secrets from me?! (*To Mystery Man*) Well go on then, spit it out.

MYSTERY MAN: The Queen is trying to kill you.

DIANA: Shut the front door.

MYSTERY MAN: It's true. She was going to have you killed in that tunnel.

DIANA: Why should I trust you?

MYSTERY MAN: I am... Someone who cares very much for you.

Mystery man takes off the sunglasses and is revealed to be...

DIANA'S DAD: It is I – Diana's Dad!

DIANA: Dad! Oh dad!

Diana runs up and hugs her dad.

DIANA: Daddy! Hang on, didn't you die 5 years ago?

DIANA'S DAD: That's not important right now.

DIANA: And you work for the Queen? You're a spy?

DIANA'S DAD: Well, we need to move the plot forward somehow.

DIANA: *(to audience, knowingly)* What plot!? *(back to Dad)* Gosh, I'm furious! If the Queen's trying to kill me, I really am in trouble. Help me dad!

DIANA'S DAD: …

DIANA: What shall I do?

DIANA'S DAD: ˉ _(◈)_/ ˉ

DIANA: Thanks a lot Dad. Hmm… The Queen can't kill me… If I kill her first.

Diana storms off.

DIANA'S DAD: If you kill her first… *(now alone on stage)* Oh my little girl. She's all grown up. *(emotional)* So very beautiful. And off to kill the Queen. As for me, I'll go back to my day job being a spy.

Diana's Dad backflips back to his seat.

31

A tense, dark version of the Queen music plays. The Queen appears on screen, flossing her teeth vigorously.

QUEEN: Hmm... Oh yes that's got it. Here I am in my room. All alone. Just me. The Queen. I am the Queen. I can't believe my plan to have Diana murdered didn't work out. I do wonder how I should have her killed instead... Maybe I'll have her join an endless queue to look at a flag covered box...

Diana enters – wearing her iconic revenge dress. Wow. What a moment.

DIANA: I'd like to see you try!

QUEEN: What?! YOU?! How did you get in here?!

DIANA: Wouldn't you like to know. How I made my way in here and past your security has an incredibly detailed and highly logical explanation, though the limited runtime of this show will not allow me to tell you it. Do you like what I'm wearing? This is my revenge dress.

QUEEN: One must admit, you are serving cunt.

DIANA: Thank you. And do you know why it's called a revenge dress?

Diana pulls out a gun.

DIANA: Because it has a gun stored in the cleavage.

The Queen gasps royally. Diana pulls out a knife.

DIANA: And a knife in the train.

The Queen gasps an even gaspier gasp. Diana pulls out a 70's style electrical meat cleaver.

DIANA: And a 70's electric meat cleaver in the derriere.

The Queen gasps the gaspiest gasp.

QUEEN: (*terrified*) No, don't kill me! I'm too young to die!

DIANA: Really?

QUEEN: Really! I still have (*checks watch*) 25 years left!

Diana raises her weapons and gets closer to the Queen.

QUEEN: (*cowering*) No! Take the corgis! Take Philip! Take Beatrice or Eugenie, or whoever they are. Just not me. I am the Queen!

Diana raises the weapons – about to strike. But instead -

DIANA: (*lowering her weapons*) I'm not going to kill you. I am a better person than that. I will let you live.

QUEEN: Wow. You really are a much better person than I will ever be.

DIANA: Yes I am. And I'm going to leave my good friend to keep an eye on you to make sure you behave. Here he is now.

Diana points. A small figure is walking into the space, greeting the audience as he enters. It's a small bear in a blue jacket and red hat.

DIANA: Hello you.

PADDY: You'd better be good now, your majesty.

QUEEN: Oh, I do hate that damn bear.

DIANA: Thank you Paddy.

PADDY: Not at all. Oh, and Diana?

DIANA: Yes?

PADDY: You really are, serving cunt.

32

Diana addresses the audience from centre stage.

DIANA: I had shown that even if the Queen tries to kill you, you don't have to kill her back. I could now live my Diana life to the fullest.

Diana exits.

33

Dramatic music plays. On the screen graphics matching the following voiceover appear.

OSCARS PRESENTER: *(offstage)* And the nominees for the Academy Award for Best Performance by an Actress in a Leading Role are:

Jennifer Hudson as Grizabella 2 in 'Cats 2: The Memory Lives... Again'

Meryl Streep as Donna Sheridan in 'Mamma Mia 3: Donna Has Risen'

and Lady Diana Spencer as Kristen Stewart in 'Stewart'

And the winner is: Lady Diana Spencer for 'Stewart'!

Diana runs on to accept her Oscar – an audience member hands her the trophy.

DIANA: Oh gosh, to think that little me was going to be here. There were three of us in this category, so it was a bit crowded. Thank you!

34

The Nobel Prize ceremony.

KING OF NORWAY: *(offstage)* Ja, as the King of Norway, it is derefore my great honour to present de Nobel Peace Prize to one of the following nominees:
Greta Thunberg for being an environmentalist hero
The people of [*name of venue*] for buying non-refundable tickets to this show
and Lady Diana for being Lady Diana.

Lady Diana appears on stage

DIANA: I really hope it's me.

KING OF NORWAY: And the winner is...the people of [*name of venue*]!

DIANA: Well, it's an honour just to be nominated alongside such wonderful people. Come on [*name of venue*] – give us a speech.

The screen feeds the speech to the audience.

AUDIENECE (*as one*): Thank you. What an honour.

DIANA: Well done!

35

DIANA: And I was the first ever cis-female former royal to compete... on RuPaul's Drag Race.

The screen shows a video of a picture of Diana "walking" down the Drag Race runway – the graphics are deliberately terrible.

DIANA (*as in a Drag Race confessional*): Oh girl, I'm stomping down the runway in my revenge dress, looking fierce. Serving house down boots mama. Opulence, I own everything - thanks to the taxpayers' money and the accident of being birthed into privilege. I'm now going to use a word I normally find quite difficult to say, because of some previous negative associations, but YAS QUEEN.

Diana clicks her fingers.

DIANA: And I also went into science, experimenting in the lab.

The screen calls Gay Scientist up from the audience.

GAY SCIENTIST: Wow Lady Di, you're so clever and intelligent.

DIANA: Well, thank you.

GAY SCIENTIST: Thank YOU for inventing PreP – it really will have the biggest effect in the fight against HIV.

DIANA: I do really want to believe that together we can eradicate AIDS within our lifetime. Undetectable equals untransmittable.

Newspapers flash up on the screen with headlines like: Diana reverses climate change, Diana stops Brexit, Diana builds 40 new hospitals, Diana named mother of the year, Diana is new chancellor – cost of living is ridiculously low! etc.

DIANA: Wow, my influence.

DIANA: So that pretty much brings us up to date. There is just one teeny tiny detail we haven't covered so far. You're probably wondering why I'm speaking to you from heaven, given that I didn't die. Let me explain. I was just at home on my own one day – applying some Elizabeth Arden cream on my lips. When suddenly...

As Diana is applying cream on her lips a voice is heard.

DIVINE VOICE: *(offstage)* Hello Diana.

DIANA: Who is that?

DIVINE VOICE: *(offstage)* It's me. The one and only. The be all and end all.

DIANA: Shawn Mendes?

GOD: No. God.

God appears on screen. She looks stunning with long shiny hair and a sparkly top.

DIANA: Oh my God...

GOD: Yes, the very same. Good to see you.

DIANA: Good to see you too. Wow – I didn't expect God to be this beautiful.

God flicks her hair.

GOD: Only very special people get to meet God you know.

DIANA: Oh, I feel so honoured.

GOD: No I'm honoured. Truth is, I'm a big fan. I've been stanning you for years. I loved you even before you got famous.

DIANA: Oh Jesus Christ.

GOD: He did too. You're probably wondering why I'm here.

DIANA: Yes, I am wondering just that.

GOD: I want to say that you are an incredible person and have done so much good for the world – and been such a fashion icon.

DIANA: Would you say I've influenced even your style?

GOD: A little. Though my main style inspiration is 2014 Eurovision Song Contest winner Conchita Wurst.

DIANA: Yes, I can see that.

GOD: Because you are so great, I am giving you something. Here you go Lady Di.

God hands a massive key to Diana.

DIANA: A key!

GOD: This is the key to heaven. With this key you can travel back and forth to heaven itself even though you're still alive. It is only given to the most special of people.

On the screen we see a montage of people travelling to heaven – the previous recipients of keys: Alison Hammond, Judi Dench, Tom Moore, Plank Lady from 'Come Dine With Me' and Vanessa Feltz.

DIANA: Even Vanessa Feltz?

GOD: Especially Vanessa Feltz.

DIANA: Thank you for the key.

GOD: It is I who should thank YOU. Ar Di. You are the best human to ever live.

DIANA: Oh, stop it.

GOD: Now sing!

An incredible pop song starts playing and Diana delivers some out-standing choreography full of references to pop divas: a bit of Gaga, Beyonce, WAP – all whilst singing:

DIANA: (*singing*)
D-I-A-N-A
I was put on the earth to slay
D-I-A-N-A

All the landmines I'll clear away
D-I-A-N-A
Come and party with me, hurray!

Born in 1961
Great ever since
One of four children
Married a prince
Popped out two babies
They are quite cute
Global fashion icon
I am a beaut

Let's go!

D-I-A-N-A
I was put on the earth to slay
D-I-A-N-A
All the landmines I'll clear away
D-I-A-N-A
Come and party with me, hurray!
D-I-A-N-A!

Diana finishes the song in a powerful pose.

Blackout.

The End.

AFTERWORD BY JOSEPH MARTIN *(who is very sexy + talented)*

Hello, I'm Joseph Martin - the other half of Awkward Productions, and Linus' fiancé (four and a half years of engagement and counting). I asked Linus if I could write an afterword for this book, and he graciously allowed it - thanks babe.

Watching Linus create this show has been nothing short of remarkable. Now, I know I'm biased, given I'm technically sleeping with the boss, but it really has been such fun working on the project. What began as a silly 60th birthday present to my Mum has become an Arts Council England funded show that has toured every nation of the UK, employed over a dozen brilliant creatives, and helped pay our rent for the best part of 8 months. Even more hilariously, it's now the published play script that you're reading right now.

I've thought of multiple things to put in this afterword when I've been just about to fall asleep, and can never remember them the following day. I should have just noted them down at the time, but rookie errors like that are probably why Linus is a published author and I am not. With that said, some of the best gags in this script are mine - see if you can spot them!

Linus commits to his madcap ideas like nobody I've ever seen. I'll go out to work for the day on whatever freelance gig I have going, and return home to find him hunched over the living room table (no matter how often I tell him to watch his posture). His first words to me won't be "Hello, how was your day?" or anything similarly affectionate, they'll be something along the lines of "So I've written this new show and I think we can probably tour it for a couple of months and then go to the fringe. I've already filled in this application, can you check it before I submit it? Also please make me dinner I'm really hungry, and then can we watch Bullseye?". I wish I was exaggerating, but I also wouldn't have it any other way.

There's a lot of ridiculously silly moments in this play, but there's also real moments of tenderness and surprisingly moving sentiments. Linus' ability to bring true heart and soul to his work is a joy to behold. He inspires me every single day to be a better version of myself. We've been together for the best part of 8.5 years now and he still keeps impressing me. Nobody in their right minds would think there was success in a) A TedTalk presentation from hell about the 2019 film 'Cats' or b) a comedy show about Lady Diana Spencer talking from heaven - fortunately, Linus absolutely isn't in his right mind and has made both of these concepts into wild successes.

I have such fun creating work with Linus. Don't get me wrong, this show is very much his baby, but building it together into what it is now has been such a ride. Getting to puppeteer Camilla Parker-Bowles every night, whilst also hearing me provide her screaming, demonic tones; in the same show that I also voice Prince Charles, Captain Sir Tom Moore, Paddy, an Oscars announcer and the King of Norway (amongst other things I've probably forgotten) is, without doubt, the strangest moment of my career to date, and I love it. Everyone should have a Linus in their lives. But you can't have my one - I'm relying on his weird brain to keep paying the rent.

I'm equal parts excited and terrified to see what we create next as Awkward Productions. This show has taken us to every part of the UK, and I have a feeling it won't stop there. Thank you to everyone that has supported us - whether that be financially, emotionally, given us a place to stay, come to see our work, told their friends, re-tweeted our endless social media content - it all means the world.

Oh, and Lady Di - I really do hope you enjoy watching this show from wherever you are, and that we've done you justice in amongst all the hilarity. You were, and are, an icon.

Thanks for reading.

Joseph x

ACKNOWLEDGEMENTS

Much love and thanks to:

Diana. This script was written as a loving celebration to you. The love and light you spread and the countless queer lives you saved and improved will never be forgotten.

Joseph - your input, love, support, humour and work on this show is everything. Both the show and I would be nothing without you.

Linda - happy birthday! To have a mother-in-law you can laugh at Diana memes with until you're both crying is one of life's biggest gifts.

Mum - your endless love and for dragging me along to various Diana exhibitions. Look what you ignited.

Dad - you are a well of kindness and my rock.

Martin, Ruby, Jay and **Bryn** - the original cast!

Amy Pitt - I asked for the near impossible and your designs were effortlessly magical.

Sam Carlyle, the choreographer and collaborator of dreams.

Wesley Maddocks for making me scream with delight over your bops and designs.

Geri Allen, the Queen of comedy.

Zina Badran, divine beyond words.

Tara Boland - the perfect mix of ridiculous and clever.

Danneh - for making videos so wonderfully stupid we cried.

Carrot - for making my Diana look so house down boots mama fierce.

Ebbe Rodtborg - My Danish lighting twink.

Dave Bird for the Di-tastic photos (including this cover!).

Nicola Williams our BSL Queen.

Chloé Nelkin, Franky Lynn and **Hannah McEwen** for spreading the #UntrueDiana gospel far and wide.

Arts Council England - thank you for believing in the project and enabling us to make this.

Alex Latham, Mia Smith, James Appleby and **Sonny Ashworth** for your help.

Ryan Ludick, Karim-Pasha Ladbon, Greg Kroll, Sean Allsop and **Sean Milne** for your incredible support.

Deborah Frances-White for being the modern day Diana.

Kestral Gaian - you amazing being! Endless gratitude for your enthusiasm and for putting me in touch with Ash.

Ash Brockwell - thank you for being so generous and kind and for helping me realise a dream I barely dared to dream.

Reconnecting Rainbows - for operating as all publishers should.

Nic, **Ellie**, **Jonny** and the amazing team at the **Pleasance**. You are stuck with us now.

Tim and **Sarah** at **Lighthouse Poole** for being the best with all your support.

Alex and **Becs** and everyone at **Old Fire Station** - the first venue to program the show, you are a dream.

Michael Miller and **Shawn Choudhury** for helping me make this Diana such a style icon.

The teams at the Alma, Theatre@41, NonSuch Studios, Town and Gown, Old Joint Stock, Òran Mór, The Brewers, The Acorn, Accidental Theatre, Two Brewers, Maddermarket and Wales Millenium Centre for believing in the work we do.

Charlotta Hansen – for endless support over the years. I love and miss you and so wish I could share this publication with you.

Jessica Lowe for being wonderful and sticking with me for so long.

Anthony Allen for friendship (and PowerPoint).

Catia Ciarico and **Karl Steele** for your support.

Johanna and **Amanda**, love you.

Joshua Goodman, our mentor.

Katharine Armitage for teaching me how to perform solo shows.

Sam Hopkins for believing I could create theatre.

Elena Liutkute and **Tom Brocklehurst** for casting me in my first play.

Swea.

My second family: **Ludde**, **Sara**, **Alva**, **Freja** och **Melker**.

Alex Young and **CDP** for igniting my creativity and feeling I could play roles way outside of my range.

Geraldyne for the playfulness and laughs.

Louis Jolly de Rosnay. Tilly Ettridge. Callum Bowyer. Matt Jordan. Gill and Alan. Matt and Mark. Chris and Ryan. Helena och Anders. Maria Block. Eva Jonsson. Terry Eastham. Maria and Stephen.

The queer community.

To **everyone** who's supported us with money, love or a place to sleep. Everyone who's bought tickets to enable this - **I thank you.**

ALSO BY RECONNECTING RAINBOWS PRESS

TransVerse, We Won't Be Erased!
Poems and Song Lyrics by Transgender and Non-Binary Writers
Edited by Ash Brockwell, 2019

TransVerse II, No Time For Silence:
Words of Survival, Resilience and Hope
Edited by Ash Brockwell, 2021

The Boy Behind The Wall:
Poems of Imprisonment and Freedom
Dalton Harrison, 2022

Counterweights
Kestral Gaian, 2022

Hidden Lives
Kestral Gaian, 2022

Emotional Literacy:
Collected Poems and Song Lyrics
Ash Brockwell, 2022

Twisted Roots
A. G. Parker, 2023

Twenty-Eight:
Stories from the Section 28 Generation
Edited by Kestral Gaian, 2023

Forthcoming:

TransVerse III, Transcendence:
Words of Faith, Love and Authenticity
Edited by Ash Brockwell

TransVerse IV, The Wait Is Killing Us:
Trans and Non-Binary People Demand Healthcare Justice!
Edited by Ash Brockwell

Potry: A Collection of Stoned Poems
Jenet La Lecheur

Songs of Remembering
Ash Brockwell